A HISTORIC GRIZZLY
The Rustlin' Rogue

Bob Nolin

Since the Lewis and Clark era, little has changed on the east slope of the Rockies of Montana, where it juts up from the eastern plains in a picturesque abrupt manner, a painter's dream. When one encompasses this setting with the Bob Marshall Wilderness to the west, the Scapegoat Wilderness to the southwest, and Glacier National Park to the northwest, I doubt if God's creation gets any more beautiful. Truly, this is wild country with mountain peaks anywhere between seven thousand and ten thousand feet above sea level. One can just imagine meadows tucked between land forms covered with alpine fir trees and whitebark (limber bark) trees that are stunted and twisted from the weight of the snow in the winter months and where the trees exposed to the wind bend in that direction, giving the landscape an unusual tint of harshness. The south slopes are exposed to more sunlight as the days lengthen and thus warm up first, which gives way to the early melting of snow. Soon after, the vegetation begins to green which makes for early spring grazing and browsing for wildlife, especially the great bear upon leaving their den. A. B. Guthrie's coined term for this total setting as the "Big Sky Country" is fitting. This land mass gives the great bears lots of room to move about, but remember they can be wandering recluses and need the space.

The east slope is home to a grizzly bear that the local ranchers know very well. A bear that will "raise havoc" with their livestock, and cost them in the tens of thousands of dollars. One can empathize with the ranchers due to the bears' depredations and their loss of property, which may never be fully realized for reimbursement because of the bears' secretive ways. The Department of Fish, Wildlife and Parks does a good job of trying to curtail grizzly problems, but their hands are tied due to government regulations, and a bear that is smart, crafty, wary, and coy. The close proximity of ranches on the east slope with a bear that is aggressive and bold, which I will call, "the east slope of Grizzlies," presents a problem! A bear will stick around as long as there is food available, and guess what? There is always food available with Montana beef grazing the countryside, and prime beef looking like sitting ducks in feed lots. The problems will continue as long as man with his livestock, and bear with its appetite, live in close proximity. Neither will be eliminated. Therefore, it is important to manage the problem bears to help eliminate livestock depredation and for the security and safety of the innocent grizzlies that can be mistaken for the perpetrators. The involvement by the federal and state governments to safely trap and relocate these bears does benefit, but is not a cure-all. Coexistence is necessary and I believe the ranchers have been more than obliging.

To help matters with this conflict, it is of vital importance that man continues to give the great bears their wilderness and not chop up portions for real estate purposes. Unfortunately, some of Montana's ranches that overlap in prime grizzly habitat, have been sold to developers, who in turn sell off lots for housing developments. At the time of this writing, two such sales were transpiring in the Madison Range. It amazes me how some people will criticize the proper management practices of hunting and logging, and then live in a house in the wilderness. Moving into their wildland habitat merely forces them further into oblivion. God has placed man in a position to properly manage animals, and we must live up to that responsibility.

Hunting is good for management purposes, if it is done with respect for proper harvest, which in turn develops a strong healthy population of game animals. It is encouraging to witness animals that were once near extinction come back because of proper hunting practices. A good illustration of this is pronghorns. At the turn of the twentieth century there were roughly twenty thousand pronghorns on the North American continent. Thanks to wise game management practices, Montana alone harvests near that amount each year. There are many more success stories due to wise hunting strategies, as developed by the state and federal Departments of Fish, Wildlife and Parks with valid input from sportsmen.

Proper logging falls into proper management too. The forests need to be thinned so the next cycle of grasses and plants may develop. These provide food for numerous animals, including the great bears. Soon underbrush develops which provides browse, especially for the ungulates. There will be buds and/or berries on the browse, which are also nutrients for birds and small game. The two-track roads developed for logging areas could be closed after the logging is over. These roads eventually grow back, but in the process are great walking, grazing and eventually browsing trails for various animals. Over many years of being in the woods I have witnessed many species of wildlife taking advantage of the foods in logged areas. Once the new growth turns to old growth, the animals all but disappear in that area. It is proven by biologists that good nutrition produces more animals, because it affects their fertility.

There will always be conflicts near or across the imaginary border that separates the grizzly habitat from man's living quarters. We have the same problem with Yellowstone National Park and their unmanaged herds, especially buffalo. They wander out of the park onto private property, which is not so bad, but they carry diseases that can contaminate cattle and sheep. I know personally, because I purchased two Blackbelly Barbados sheep from a gentleman near Gardiner, a town that borders Yellowstone to the north. They eventually died from para-tuberculosis and the carriers were the buffalo, according to the Montana State laboratory in Bozeman. We know they also carry brucellosis.

Some people want to buy the adjoining private ranches to Yellowstone Park so there is a neutral zone. If this happens then the buffalo eventually will leave this new point of demarcation, and then we are back to the very same problem. Whenever man and beast come together there will be problems eventually. In the particular case of this book, the problem is between the east slope grizzlies and ranches. Grizzlies, unlike buffalo, do not carry diseases that can contaminate cattle, they just outright kill the cattle. Having the great bears in your backyard is like sitting on a keg of dynamite and it is just a matter of time before a confrontation develops between man and beast. In some cases the problem can be corrected without further harm, but in the case of some bears the problem may persist for years. The aggressive east slope grizzlies are a challenge and in the minds of different ranchers and Department of Fish, Wildlife and Parks personnel the problem started with one bear! This book will hone in on that one bear and as you read the next chapters, I believe you will testify that this bear was very unusual and unique and that it was in a class of its own!

Chapter 1
A Sow Gives Birth

In 1981 a sow gave birth, perhaps to two cubs, since this the most common number. The den was in a remote and blizzardy area, for snow to cover her entrance during the long winter's hibernation. It was located on a steep incline so there would be a solid roof, yet not too steep so the snow could not cover the entrance. A thirty degree pitch seems to be near average and on the leeward, where the snow accumulates. The den was anywhere from six thousand to ten thousand feet in elevation above sea level. In April the sow emerged first, followed by her cubs to a new world. The cubs had been nursing and napping since January and were near five pounds when they emerged from the dark and into the light, signifying their debut of the intense learning process from their mother. Success in life will depend on what they learn in the next couple of years while with her. Regardless of similar upbringing, each cub will learn, and display, different behavioral traits because they are individuals, much like humans.

The mother bear will teach the cubs how to respond to different stimuli, such as threatening situations. There is little doubt that the cubs will react differently to the same stimulus before mother's conditioning

Photo by Jim & Tony Hamilton, Cody, WY

prevails. For example, my son and I were black bear hunting when we spotted a sow grizzly with cubs walking toward us at one hundred and fifty yards distance. She spotted us and gave a warning to the two cubs. Already the cubs were showing individual differences, in that, one of the cubs immediately headed for the timber while the other cub kept nonchalantly walking our way. The mother immediately swatted the cub turning it head over heels. I am sure that would not happen next time at the onset of danger for that cub. Even at this early age, Ladd and I saw a wariness with one cub and a boldness with the other. But for the most part, the cubs will be good observers and responders as they watch their mother respond to different situations, and will mimic her. They will learn when, where and how to acquire food. Eating of various vegetation at different times of the year will be ever-learned. Watching their mother smell out carrion from great distances and approach it cautiously, and in some cases boldly, will register with them. They will watch her chase predators off carrion to claim or reclaim it, and learn that this rotten meat feels good to the stomach and digests well. They will learn to dig and roll rocks in pursuit of rodents for a nutritious protein meal. Getting into bee hives, ant hills, and learning when and where to eat moths will become a practice as well.

How to stalk and kill larger game, like elk, will be learned but not practiced until they become of age. Throughout their learning years they become more bold and begin to realize they dominate other animals. Indeed they are the "King of the Beasts."

The cubs also learn about their two enemies: boar grizzlies and man. They are being educated to avoid both, and mother grizzly shows them that the night hours are safer from man. Nocturnal activity becomes a way of life, while the daylight hours are spent resting. If they inhabit areas that are undisturbed by man then they will feed at different times during the day, but normally this occurs before dark, and right at daylight.

These cubs were definitely groomed in the wilderness and not in one of Montana's national parks, where hoards of people visit each year, causing cubs, to some extent, to become familiar with people. It is more likely that the twosome hardly saw man.

The other enemy, the boar grizzly, may try to separate the cubs from their mother so they can kill and eat them, regardless of the time of day. The cubs will learn how to climb trees to avoid this enemy, but as they mature this will not be necessary. In fact the structure of their claws, as they develop, will make it very difficult to climb. Besides separating the cubs from their mother, boars have been known to dig the cubs out of their den, when hungry, while the mother is in a lethargic state, but this is rare. The sow will protect her cubs with ferocity since she does not have cubs but every three years or so, and not until she is mature, which is around five years of age. Instinctively she will keep close watch over them as they learn through her example.

My son, Ladd, lives in Anchorage, Alaska and shared an interesting story with me that happened on the north slope, above the Brooks

Photo by Jim & Tony Hamilton, Cody, WY

Range. There were five polar bears feeding on a whale carcass on the shore, I believe in or near Prudeau Bay. An inland grizzly with cubs chased the five polar bears off the carcass, then she and the cubs claimed the prize. Those cubs learned the respect their mother has, even with animals three times her size. One day they will do the same thing, because they were trained in this process. She, no doubt, was a little more owly and protective because of the cubs, and would defend them at any cost.

The cubs are ever-learning as they mature, learning how to avoid danger, to locate food, where to go for shelter, and how to have fun. They will scuffle, slide down snow embankments, chase bugs, birds, and about any small animal they see move. Their skills are being honed for the day they will be on their own.

Their first encounter with man could have been hikers, campers or hunters in the wilderness. They watched their mother's reaction of avoiding this new creature and soon learned to copy it. Besides learning this behavior, there was something about man that made them wary and uncomfortable (unbeknown to them that God instilled this in them from the very beginning, Genesis 1:26-28).

One of the cubs, even at an early age, would show signs of independence and boldness. At what age, and why this cub began to step outside the norm, one can only speculate. Like people, some bears are known to be leaders (alphas) and some followers. This cub was surely destined to be different, because its leadership was beginning to emerge and with all the necessary characteristics that are pertinent. When and how this cub learned that cattle and man associate, and that it was possible to choose the time and place to assault cattle without man knowing, can also be speculated.

Chapter 2
The Cubs are Maturing

In June of their third year, the sow came in heat, and it was time for mating. The sow, in her natural way, became stern with the cubs (now sub-adults), and did not want them around. She was acting unmotherly and because of her stressful mood swings the cubs set off on their own. They had been trained by their mother but now they needed to apply what they had learned. They would also learn new behavior under different circumstances. No doubt these juveniles would get into trouble, especially the bold one. Whatever happened to one cub is a mystery, but we will follow the other cub, a female. In her pursuit of food, especially protein, she became a wanderer preferring the east slope of the Rockies. Most grizzlies stay in the wilderness, but she was different. Because of her free spirit she headed east and found animals to her liking that resembled the familiar elk. Because of her mother's example and within her grizzly being she knew that she could overpower these strange animals. She saw that they were not as wild and that she could easily catch them. So it became no challenge, and she killed her first beef. The taste and satisfaction was nothing like she had ever experienced. When she had watched her mother kill an elk and they devoured it as a family, only that might rival this gourmet meal of beef. This whole ordeal of killing on her own seemed to fit her disposition, and she was not going to change. She definitely was setting the stage for herself and other grizzlies, because she was the alpha and the other grizzlies would watch as she killed, eventually they would follow her influence. But she had not yet been adept to man's tricks and would soon learn the hard way.

The following is a question I had and still have: Was she an heir to the Lewis and Clark grizzly that was pushed from eastern and central Montana to the Rocky Mountains? In other words, did her genetics dictate that she be a plains bear, by finding the foothills and the open parks on the east slope to be more of a conducive atmosphere than the forests in the wilderness? She seemed to like the openness, yet she stayed close enough to brush and the thick forest for safety.

Enough is mentioned about the grizzlies in early history to know they were bold and caused a lot of concern and problems. The early trappers faced a lot of hardships as they

Photo by Jim & Tony Hamilton, Cody, WY

collected furs, especially beaver, for the various fur companies. They faced cold, wind, heat, frigid waters, isolation, guerrilla warfare and competition. As if these were not enough, the mountain men had to face the great bear. Some experts speculate that the most aggressive bears died with the mountain men. Their journals are saturated with gory clashes, and it appears that the bear of yesteryear was bolder and more cantankerous. They wrote of the grizzly as a horrible monster that would rather kill a man than run from him. These early descriptions of the great bear earned it the scientific name, "Ursus horribilis," with Montana's subspecies listed as "Ursus arctos horribilis." When Captain Meriwether Lewis was run off his buffalo kill and into the Missouri River, it became a good illustration of the boldness and feistiness of Ursus arctos horribilis. Our young grizzly displayed similar boldness and feistiness. More will be said of these characteristics later on. Besides favoring the openness of the east slope and her boldness and feistiness, a third reason I feel she might be a descendant of the Lewis and Clark heir, is that she became very interested in cattle. Could the cattle possibly be the substitute for buffalo? Is there an innate desire to go after larger animals, which her gene pool dictates? We may never know the answers to these questions, but they are intriguing thoughts.

I want to share another thought with you, the reader, that is very interesting. As the three-year-old was maturing and her hair was become more pronounced, she was becoming darker around her eyes, legs and flanks. Many colorations of hair were distributed throughout her whole body, for a grand total of seven colors! She became a calico colored specimen with the following colors: black, white, silver tip, orange, blond, cinnamon and brown. Her hump was becoming noticeably darker too. It was almost unimaginable to fathom a bear with so many beautiful markings, but the trait I will focus on is her face mask, which resembles a raccoon appearance. With that in mind I have another question: Could she be a product from British Columbia? I had an acquaintance who lived in Cranbrook, B.C. and after he saw a picture of this bear he commented that there is an area in B.C. that possesses a population of bears with similar face markings. He should know because he had been a guide for years and was very knowledgeable concerning grizzlies. Could this young grizzly have migrated from that great distance? Maybe her ancestors came from there. These are very interesting thoughts that one may never know the answers to, yet could there some truth to them?

Regardless of her heritage, she was a roamer and was on the move constantly in search of food. She had such endless energy and seemed like she needed to vent it somehow. Maybe she found a certain amount of security in her wanderings. I doubt whether she stayed very long in any one location, which was proven by her pattern, and she seemed to be so inbred with this desire that she would never change. This would prove to be an asset for her and a liability for man, as she was predictable in being unpredictable. Roaming ten miles per day was hardly an effort for her, but to where, was the question.

The future was approaching when she would be the ring leader to a problem that would forever change the reputation of the east slope grizzlies. This problem would begin with this beautiful, bold and rogue grizzly in the eyes of many. She would become publicized throughout the country.

Chapter 3
The Perpetrator

In the Mid 1980's I read about a grizzly taking down cattle in feedlots near Augusta, Montana on the east slope of the Rockies. The bear would kill, eat what it wanted, then leave and never return. This presented a problem for both the ranchers and the Department of Fish, Wildlife and Parks. The ranchers were losing cattle in their own feedlots in close proximity to their homes, besides in the pastures where the cattle grazed. One night the killings would take place close to Augusta and shortly thereafter a similar assault on cattle would take place near Choteau. The Lord only knows how many grazing cattle were killed in the mountains by the perpetrator. This whole scenario was presenting a problem and the public began an outcry, thus the Departments (state and federal) had a problem too.

Why this particular bear began the cattle killing business is anybody's guess. This grizzly killed other livestock too, but cattle seemed to be her preference. The beef protein was addicting and she seemed to go to extremes, just like an addict, to get it. The bear was listening to it's God–given instincts of dominance over other animals, even animals two and three times her weight! Normally killing animals of great size is not the first preference of a meal for a grizzly. They seem to prefer carrion, rodents or any meal that takes less energy. They do not want to burn needed energy, as the great bears are readying themselves for the winter den. All summer they make preparation for hibernation and will need the necessary body fat to get them through the winter. So why would a grizzly want to expend more energy and fat content than necessary? Maybe the killing was so quick and effective that it did not require much energy? This is rather a sobering thought, isn't it? If you were one of the ranchers with such an animal habituating and killing your cattle, what could it do to you unaware? How would you feel from day to day as you worked the ranch? "Uneasy," might be a good term.

The bear was more nocturnal in its killings, especially around ranch buildings. Normally the wiser, older grizzly tend to stay away from the daylight hours because of the dangers inherent with man. This grizzly seemed to be coy and cunning near people, but feed indiscriminately during daylight hours when and where there was no threat. She was behaving like an old experienced grizzly!

Both of our great parks, Glacier and Yellowstone, have people infringing on the great bears on a regular basis. Because of these interruptions, the park bears have grown accustomed to people, and they will feed during the day to a greater extent than the non-park grizzlies that live in close proximity to people. At least this has been my observation. On occasion a grizzly gets hacked off, and man is always on the losing end of the encounter. The public quickly learns about the happening and then public opinions become rampant. Whether the bear is caught or not, it is determined if there will be any further danger. If so, then the hunt begins, if not, then the bear is left alone. My personal bias is this: that anyone who enters these parks is at risk and if they do not like the risk they should stay home. However, if a bear does present a continuous problem then it must be removed. This is where the east slope grizzly fits in. This single bear, along with its followers, continuously presented a problem to the ranchers. To remove the perpetrators, especially this perpetrator was necessary. The task at hand would not be easy, in fact it was difficult and I was called on to do it! This will come later, but first let us examine a couple stories of grizzlies that became fearless of man, since this attribute seemed applicable to this grizzly.

Roscoe, a man I know who managed the St. Mary's Lodge at St. Mary's, Montana was walking a high mountain trail in Glacier National Park with two lady friends. One of the ladies stayed behind to take pictures while Roscoe and the other lady continued their sightseeing adventure. The two of them rounded a corner on the trail, when out of nowhere a grizzly knocked Roscoe down and began to throw him around like a rag doll. He told me that he was helpless. As the bear was mauling him the lady ran to a tree and began to ascend. By doing this she actually saved Roscoe, because the bear left him in his blood and torn body and sprinted for the tree. The grizzly reached up near ten feet and grabbed the lady by her gastrocnemius muscle (calf) and jerked her out of the tree. While doing so, the bear had folded the muscle over her ankle! As she lay there in pain and shock, the bear just sniffed her and turned and walked off. Apparently the mood swing was over. Roscoe, who is a larger person, perhaps two hundred and fifty pounds with a six foot four inch frame, told me the bear was no bigger than him, yet threw him around with very little effort! What strength! Why did this bear do that? Was it tired of people invading its territory? Was it startled? Was it a sow with cubs, although no cubs were spotted? Apparently it was not hungry, otherwise one would reason that the two of them would have been a gourmet's delight. We can conclude that the bear was fearless of man because of its nonchalant attitude. It was more accustomed to man and the many interruptions, unlike the wilderness bears. The other lady, after taking pictures, resumed her hike and came upon her two companions! She ran for help and soon a helicopter from Kalispell's Regional Hospital came to their rescue. I do not know about the lady, but Roscoe has scars to prove his story.

Another person I know from Columbia Falls, Montana was returning from a day's fishing on Quartz Lake. He was walking a trail to his vehicle, when out of nowhere a grizzly came in hot pursuit of him. Tony had a Mepps Spinner on the end of his rod and was holding the rod backwards with the handle to the front. The evening was setting in and he did not take the time to put the hook in his tackle box. As fate would have it, the bear lunged for Tony and got the Mepps Spinner hook stuck in its nose. Because the nose is a sensitive area, the bear gave up its pursuit and bolted for the timber. The last thing Tony saw was the grizzly running with a rod and real dangling behind. Although this is rather a comical story, one thing is for certain, the bear appeared to be fearless of man.

Photo by Jim & Tony Hamilton, Cody, WY

In these two stories both of these bears were park bears and they appeared more bold around people than their counterpart, that is, the non-park bears who very seldom see people. One very seldom reads of bear maulings outside of the National parks today. But the east slope grizzly is presenting itself as very bold and brazen, even within man's reach! They are getting too close for comfort, with man being unaware for the most part! That is scary! To think that brute beasts are lurking around the ranches in search of food and right next door to living quarters! Indeed, the east slope grizzlies were becoming bold in their killings. They killed in feedlots, tied up animals, and animals that had been properly groomed for 4-H projects. To make matters worse, the bears were led by the fearless one! Because of this bear and her followers, not only were the livestock in harm's way, but man, being in close proximity to these fearless bears, had to be ever alert!

Chapter 4
Bear Facts

Years past I read that the inland grizzly is the most respected by those who have hunted the four most feared bears. That list includes the Alaska brown, polar, Russian brown and the inland grizzly, (which is the classification of the east slope grizzlies). It is very interesting that the inland grizzly would be placed above the other three since it is generally the smallest of the cousins. When a person considers its total package of characteristics it makes sense. Those characteristics consist of temperament, speed, power, strength, intelligence, quickness, boldness, resilience, unpredictability, cunning and craftiness, wariness and finally a sixth sense. Not that the other three bears lack any of these, but it seems the interior grizzlies rely on their package more. Consequently, these bears are considered formidable foes.

The great bear's temperament can come across in such a way that it may fight or flee in an instant. Often it will bluff charge or it might charge and not bluff. One just never knows, because its temperament can change. For example, my first grizzly encounter put me into a most insecure predicament. As I rounded a game trail there standing before me, only 25 feet away, was a large boar grizzly! We immediately had a staring contest. Suddenly he began to throw his large head from side to side, which can be a sign that he is coming! For some unknown reason the bear quit throwing his head, looked at me, and just walked off the trail nonchalantly. Why the change! Who knows, but his mood changed, signifying its unpredictable temperament. I believe the Lord watched out for me.

On another occasion I watched a grizzly walk undisturbed and then for no apparent reason quickly tear into some sapling trees to shred them. Why the outburst in such short order? This type of temperament makes the great inland grizzlies very unpredictable and dangerous.

When one talks of animals with speed it always drifts to the cheetah or pronghorn. But to watch a large burly animal that can run over thirty-five miles per hour is impressive! I have witnessed one run down a healthy elk. I have heard it said that a grizzly would outrun a racehorse for the first one hundred yards or so. Imagine a grizzly in a chute at the Kentucky Derby and when the gates open the great bear is out in front of all those thoroughbreds! Wow! A top sprinter in track will cover about thirty-two to thirty-five feet per second, while a grizzly will cover more than forty-five feet per second.

The power of a grizzly is second to none. To illustrate this, a man, whom I know, was mauled by a grizzly after lifting the gate of a culvert trap as he released the bear. In seconds the bear was out, pulled the trap off the flatbed and caused Louis, who was positioned on top, to slide down the top length of the trap onto the bear! The power, strength and speed to do all this in the short time it took Louis to hustle from the front to the back of the culvert trap is amazing! This occurrence greatly impressed two outdoor writers who were witnessing the release. One said afterwards that he had heard of the great bear's power and strength and its amazing feats, but he could not digest it all. After this episode he said there is no comparison between a black bear and a grizzly, since he was only familiar with black bears. Now he is a believer in Ursus arctos horribilis' power and strength.

A friend of mine was a guide in the Bob Marshall Wilderness. While packing with horses along a trail that paralleled a cliff, one of the pack horses slipped and catapulted several hundred feet to the bottom. Doug climbed down to claim all the gear, and decided that the dead horse would serve as bait for a grizzly. Knowing there were grizzlies in the area, he waited high above the horse through the night with the necessary equipment and gear in anticipation of an opportunity at daylight. As the sun lifted in the eastern sky, Doug carefully studied the landscape below, only to discover the horse was missing! He was totally bewildered as to what happened to the horse! Doug climbed down the cliff and found that the horse was dragged a couple hundred yards to the Middle Fork of the Flathead River by a grizzly! Doug waded the river and continued following the drag marks, which led to a huge bear cache! After carefully surveying the sight he decided against any more grizzly hunting. The one thing that stood out in his mind was the awesome strength of an animal that was able to drag a mountain horse that distance!

My father-in-law and brother-in-law were on a fishing trip to the peninsula of Alaska. One night a grizzly took their fifty-five gallon drum that was sealed with garbage and bent it like a pop can! Immense strength is almost an understatement. They decided that moving on might be their best proposition.

When it comes to intelligence, I doubt if there is an animal alive that can outwit the great bear. It does not take a grizzly long to determine danger, thus becoming nocturnal to avoid any mishaps. This is especially true in Alaska during hunting season. Tony Russ in his "Bear Hunting in Alaska" book said that the large boars figure out what is happening right away and can only be found a few minutes after daybreak and immediately before dark. I can testify to this statement since I had firsthand experience while on the Alaskan peninsula.

Although the east slope grizzlies were only hunted on a very restricted basis, they knew to remain coy and elusive because of the strained relationship with man. Traps were set for these rogue bears that rustled cattle, but quite often the traps were of no avail because these bears figured them out, regardless of the temptation of the bait. The traps that the Department of Fish, Wildlife and Parks use are called culvert traps because they were originally built of road culverts. Today they are custom-welded of aluminum alloys, but still resemble the old culvert traps. Grizzlies reason the danger of the traps more so than black bears, and because of this, the Department of Fish, Wildlife, and Parks will use a snare that is made of airplane-grade steel and anchored to a strong secure tree. This will work for a while then its effectiveness is lost as the bear figures this out too. Ben Long mentions in his book, "Great Montana Bear Stories," that both snares and culvert traps are humane in comparison with the old number 5 Newhouse grizzly trap. It was approximately four feet long and the open jaws spread about twenty inches in diameter. A heavy chain was used to anchor the trap to a tree. When the bear would step on the scentless trap that was covered lightly with debris, the trap would jump as the jaws closed, and teeth would penetrate the flesh. It was impossible to pull the trap off the leg—not very humane, but dangerously effective. With these brief examples one should be left with the thought that the grizzly is an intelligent animal. Only man with his ingenious mind can devise plans to outwit Ursus arctos horribilis, but not in all cases. Other examples of intelligence will be given throughout the remainder of the book.

Nothing amazes me more than the homing instinct of the grizzlies! They can be trapped, drugged and hauled for several hundred miles while groggy, turned around, and basically blind-folded by the culvert trap in which they have limited vision, then find their way back to where it all began! It does not take them months or years, but only days, regardless of the terrain!

A retired B.L.M. (Bureau of Land Management) person I know did some trapping of grizzly bears to relocate them. They did most of their trapping near the Canadian border and close to the North Fork of the Flathead River. He told me that one of the bears they trapped traveled almost two hundred miles back to its hangout. It took this bear only a couple of weeks to do so and over some of the worst terrain! I heard that the joke amongst the Department of Fish, Wildlife and Parks is that the released bear will be back to where it was trapped before the Department's personnel who trapped the bear will be home. The great bears have a sense of direction and the way God instilled this in them is just amazing!

When it comes to quickness the grizzlies are anything but second. I saw footage of two grizzlies standing toe to toe with their paws gouging each other and their mouths biting out chunks of flesh, all done with amazing quickness. Their motions were so fast that in slow motion it was quick! Spit and fur were flying every direction as they brawled! When they kill an animal larger than themselves, quickness is an asset in addition to strength. Just ask Louie when the grizzly bolted out of the trap, grabbed it, and pulled it down before Louie could clear himself as he ran on top of the trap! It only took seconds for all this to transpire! Speed, running over thirty-five miles per hour, is one thing, but body explosion quickness is another!

Years ago I witnessed a line of men trying to turn a grizzly over on a mat, much like two wrestlers. If they were able to do so, then they would be awarded a monetary prize. The grizzly with the command by the trainer stood on all fours. The person would put his one hand on the bear's front upper leg and his other over the bear's back. Weight was no factor since this bear was hardly any bigger than these two hundred and fifty pound people. On a command from the trainer the scuffle started, and in a matter of seconds the bear was on top of each one of the contestants. One guy apparently irritated the bear because the bear flew up and around in one motion and had the guy pinned! It was a blessing the bear was declawed and wore a face muzzle, or this guy would have been in big trouble. I could hardly believe the quickness of that bear!

In Monterrey, Mexico a California grizzly killed an African lion so quickly that the large crowd watching did not know how it was done! During that same time frame a grizzly killed a bull in a ring in similar fashion.

Boldness is another characteristic of the grizzly. It fears only man and in many cases has learned to adjust to man, which can be dangerous when within close proximity. They have walked into campsites and dragged people out of their tents to kill them, or kill and eat them. Sometimes they just walk into camp and watch as people scatter. On different occasions I had grizzlies just look at me and not run, but walk away or just continue to eat with little concern. On many occasions I watched grizzlies continue to graze, knowing full well that I was watching. In Montana, and as far away as the Brookes Range in Alaska, I witnessed this boldness. The bear's indifference and boldness are not desirable attributes when it comes to man's safety.

Concerning their resilience, if one has an opportunity to shoot while hunting a grizzly, the first shot must be put into the heart and lung area. I agree with Tony Russ in his book, "Bear Hunting in Alaska," when he said just keep shooting after that first fatal shot. Because of the great bear's resilience, it normally takes more than one shot. My son and I witnessed this when we hunted brown bear (large grizzlies) on the Alaskan peninsula. They can and will survive under the most duress conditions physically, while other animals would die.

There are many such stories of grizzlies that survived, when in all reality they should not have. One such story is that of Lenny, "the bulletproof bear," as told in "The Great Montana Bear Stories," by Ben Long. A hunter wounded Lenny at point-blank range while the hunter was elk hunting. The hunter stumbled across the bear in thick brush and, figuring it was going to charge, he shot three times. Two bullets struck Lenny's shoulder and the third went right through him in the mid section. The bear hurried away leaving a blood trail. The hunter told the authorities and they followed the blood trail that showed signs of being shot, not only in muscle and bone, but in the guts. A gut-shot animal will die a slow agonizing death. The game wardens followed the 30-06 shot bear for several miles. The bear kept going so they gave up chase to not hamper the bear any further. Lenny eventually went into hibernation and according to the telemetry reading he was still alive. Since Lenny was radio collared they could keep tabs on him throughout the winter. In the spring, Lenny came out and was eventually captured. The wardens simply could not believe that Lenny survived! His wounds were healed over and he was healthy once again. Eventually he lost his collar and was unseen for years. Finally a warden, who was flying over the Cabinet Mountains, saw Lenny feeding in the high country.

In 1988 a young grizzly was trapped in the South Fork of the Flathead. It had a fist-sized wound in one of the back legs and a huge chunk of flesh was bitten out of the bear's rump. A large boar also bit the smaller grizzly in the nose and punctured one of the eyes causing blindness. A hole was punctured below the eye so when the bear breathed, air would go in and out like a third nostril. The bear was later named "Popeye." When "Popeye" was reexamined some time later, its rump was completely healed! He was tough and very resilient!

Grizzlies do adapt extremely well to various food and food sources. Their menu includes: roots, plants, grasses, clover, dandelions, honey, bark, small and large animals, garbage, seeds, fish, carrion, black bears,

other grizzlies, etc. They will be cannibalistic and eat their own. This was very obvious when my son and I were hunting brown bear on the Alaskan peninsula. We scoped boars high up in the snowfield as they searched for dens to dig into and get the cubs. Every boar harvested by a hunter saves cubs from this early death.

They will find food in some of the most unique areas too. For example, in the Mission Mountains of Montana there is a location where moths migrate during the month of August. I am not sure if it is to breed or reproduce, but regardless, they are a source of food for grizzlies. The bears know where and when and will travel for miles to gourmandize. How did the great bears ever figure out that moths would be a source of protein and where and when to find them in great numbers?

In 1997 a grizzly was live-trapped near the North Fork of the Flathead in northwest Montana. When this bear was released elsewhere she found easy food from bird feeders, horse feed, and human food. She knew exactly where to go to find the food, without ever being in that country. It seems wherever the grizzlies are planted, they are so resilient in their choice of food that they will not starve. Being omnivorous is evident in grizzlies.

Another bear that I heard of some years ago was hassling an outfitter by eating their elk and deer kills. The outfitter built a solid log cabin to serve as the cache. The peak of the roof was eight feet and it would slope to six feet. It was strong and weather proof, but not grizzly proof. The door was built so it would swing out like a typical front door. One night the midnight marauder found a way to break in. He took his powerful claws and grabbed the edge of the door and pulled it open. He proceeded to feast on elk and deer quarters. The outfitter then figured he would outfox the grizzly by building the door reverse so the crafty bear could not get his claws in the crack and pull it open thinking there was just no place for the grizzly to hook his claws. Because the bear is so resilient, he quickly dealt with the change. He went to the roof and pushed it up like a weight lifter at the six feet roof line. He pushed the roof off the anchors on the one side, then climbed up and in and got his fill. Rather than go back up and over, he grabbed the door with his powerful claws and jerked it open to the inside and walked out. Not only resilient, but smart and crafty, maybe even a little rebellious?

Have you heard of the sixth sense of a grizzly bear? I have seen it, and it is downright frightening! My hunting buddy and I were high on a mountain ridge overlooking a plush green meadow, near four hundred yards distance, waiting for a black bear to come and feed. There was a strong updraft which was not swirling. We sat very quietly and blended well amongst the rocks. Within ten minutes emerged the largest inland grizzly that I have ever seen. It was a monster of a bear! The bear proceeded to feed and within five minutes lifted its head and looked in our direction! He continued to feed and then a minute or so later lifted his head and looked our way! This went on for the better part of half an hour. That bear knew we were there, but how? He could not smell us, he could not hear us, he could not see us, as we were blended in, practically hiding. That bear just sensed us with a mysterious "sixth sense!"

On another occasion I was stalking a cinnamon black bear, at least that is what I thought. The breeze was strong in my face, the stalk was quiet and the bear could not see me, but I knew his whereabouts. As I moved within one hundred yards, the bear moved away from me to hide. He knew danger was lurking, so he quickly melted into some timber and brush. The bear turned out to be a grizzly boar when I finally had a good view of him! He could not see me, smell me, or hear me, but he knew! (It was that "sixth sense"—I just know it!) Had I known it was a grizzly there is no way I would have stalked him, even with my 300 Magnum in hand. People who have observed the great bear numerous times will confirm its uncanny awareness that someone is around, a deep seated feeling that something is not right, again it has to be that "sixth sense!"

I put the cunningness of the grizzlies as yet another characteristic of Ursus arctos horribilis. Cunningness can be part of intelligence, yet I feel it deserves a separate consideration. Maybe it is putting intelligence into practical use, like the bear pushing the roof of the cache, eating the meat and then pulling the door open to the inside and walking out!

The case of the Giefer bear shows, not only intelligence but cunningness too. In 1976 this bear continued his habit of breaking into cabins for easy meals. He especially liked Smucker's Strawberry Jam. The cabin owners became frustrated, so they put spikes in plywood and placed their invention in front of doors and over windows. This did not stop the Giefer bear, because he learned to bend the spikes and continue ransacking. The wardens caught the bear and relocated it up the North Fork of the Flathead in northwest Montana wearing a radio collar. The Giefer was attracted to more cabins in the North Fork, and a bunch of new caches! The wardens even set a table feast for the bear by bringing road kills and dropping them off at certain locations to distract the cunning and smart bear from cabins and Smucker's Strawberry Jam. Hauling these road kills up the washboard gravel road continued all summer. As it turned out the bear did not like government handouts, he was not lazy and wanted to earn his keep. He ended up breaking into over a dozen cabins and the North Fork people were irate! Finally, after public pressure the wardens were forced to catch the bear and put it down. One would think that a radio-collared grizzly would be easy to catch up with. From experience this is not so, and it takes the right conditions, and, believe me, the right breaks too!

The wardens got lots of help and took for the mountains after the elusive bear. Pilots even flew overhead to relay the whereabouts of the Giefer bear to the land crew. The bear was on the move constantly, which can be typical for grizzlies. The wardens were always one step behind the wily bear. To make matters worse they would receive another irate phone call that the bear had broken into yet another cabin! The bear was hard to track and always one step ahead. Now he had broken into fifty-five cabins and he even hit some cabins twice! The wardens were looking like a bunch of keystone cops. This bear was so smart and cunning that he must have had a doctor's degree, one warden related to a local newspaper reporter. At one cabin the bear ripped down the outside door, yet opened the cupboard doors gently. At another cabin it looked like the Giefer bear slept on a cot, much like the papa bear in children's books. Trappers, wardens, biologists, and members of the sheriff's posse were very frustrated! They set baits, attractive baits at that, but the bear just looked at them, even for long periods of time, but never took them. The bear was compared to Jesse James and Butch Cassidy. The North Fork people kept their loaded firearms at arm's length in wait for the robber. As fate would have it, more bad luck followed for the people and good luck for the Giefer. When the bear broke into another cabin, he caught his collar on a nail and pulled it off! Now the problem seemed unsolvable.

Finally, the "Feds" came and were going to show the state personnel how to capture this grizzly—with a cocky attitude and all the disposition that goes with it. Sure enough the Feds caught the large male grizzly and accidentally overdosed it. Now the people of the North Fork felt bad that the robber was dead, even though he hampered so many of them. They had sided with the bear over the government, especially the cocky bunch that was sent in. Well, the story does not end here, because in their haste they forgot to look inside the lip. There was no tattoo, which the Giefer possessed! They had captured and killed the wrong bear! The locals were now cheering, since the Giefer outfoxed them once again. The Feds packed up and left and everyone cheered! The Giefer went silent for several weeks and even the locals were concerned that someone had poached him. There was a plea for someone to admit to it and that they would not be squealed on, but there was no response. Just before denning up the Giefer struck again! He hit a couple more cabins and then went into hibernation. Everyone was relieved, happy and the frustration turned into cheering!

Unfortunately, the Giefer went across the Canadian border the next spring where hunting is legal, and was shot by a hunter with a guide. The people of the North Fork were sad when they heard the report, yet relieved that their cabins would once again be unharmed. I would call this bear very cunning, crafty, cagey and smart, wouldn't you agree? This story is from "Great Montana Bear Stories," by Ben Long.

My son and I were caribou hunting in Alaska, and after a morning of hunting we decided to spend the afternoon in camp, cleaning things up and resting for the evening hunt. As I surveyed the landscape across a small lake we were camped by, a grizzly materialized. The bear was feeding on blueberries and seemed very content. In a matter of seconds the bear changed from being content to being on edge. It turned, looked downhill, stood very erect, then quickly made itself unknown in some brush. We studied the direction in which the bear was alerted. In minutes we saw three caribou hunters slowly moving up the long hill. Eventually they walked right by the brush the grizzly was in, having no idea the great bear was holed up only fifty feet away. They did not know, but the bear knew! Wow! How cunning and crafty that bear was. I had to wonder right then and there—how many times had I walked by a grizzly while hunting, fishing or hiking?

When it comes to prudence in detecting and escaping danger, I cannot think of an animal as wary. When you observe a grizzly, whether it be feeding or just doing its thing, they are always cautious. It is very alert to any kind of danger, always staying in close proximity to timber and brush for escape and protection. The vast majority of time the bear will detect people first, with the person having no idea that the great bear had just been there. Many times I found fresh bear scat, not even aware I had been detected! Talk about an eerie feeling!

"Predictably unpredictable" is another characteristic that I saw in the female bear that is called "The Rustlin' Rogue." Like the Giefer bear, it would only be a matter of time before an assault would happen (predictable), but where and when were the questions (unpredictable). Cattle were the victims and not cabins.

Chapter 5
Bear #316

When the Department of Fish, Wildlife and Parks captured the female bear she was three years old and roaming with a male that was three years her senior. The Department determined this because he was captured a few days later looking for his mate. The male was given the number "346," and he would become a legend in his own time, called "The Falls Creek Grizzly!" The female became numbered "316," and people soon learned that she was the instigator and leader of the east slope grizzlies during this time. The two of them

Photo by Bob Nolin, Billings, MT

turned to livestock killing, primarily cattle, and under the influence of this female bear called "The Rustlin' Rogue." She possessed all the characteristics as found in Chapter 4: temperamental, speed, power, strength, intelligence, quickness, boldness, resilience, unpredictability, cunningness and craftiness, wariness and that "sixth sense!" Wrapping all these attributes into an animal, particularly a grizzly and specifically "The Rustlin' Rogue," put a lot of concern and enormous frustration in the minds and emotions of those people who had to deal with her! Had she lived longer there is no doubt that she would be talked about in hunting camps where grizzlies are the topic, although she still is in some camps!

Let us pick her story up as found in the book, "Great Montana Bear Stories" by Ben Long. A biologist in the 1970's and 80's became very knowledgeable about telemetry science, ideal for use on the east slope. He set foot snares on Bill Mosher's ranch in May of 1985. His ranch is located where the mountains and prairies adjoin. There were two grizzlies, a male and female, paying the ranch frequent visits. The biologist set snares in the Cuniff Creek area with tempting bait to catch the grizzlies, so that he could radio collar them and keep tracking records. The three-year-old female was the first to fall for the trick. The male, in days to come, was lured in by the trapper's cunningness to use the female's powerful pheromones, since it was mating season. It worked and he was also fitted with a collar. He became #346 and she became #316. He was six years of age and she was three. Now they would be tracked to determine if they were the cattle killers. Within a short period of time word went out that more cattle bit the dust and that #316 was the culprit. She was so bold that she was caught three times killing cattle on the east slope cattle ranches. The Department of Fish, Wildlife and Parks set her free miles away from the kill sites, only to have her return to kill more. She was so bold that she blew all caution to the wind to the Department's creative trapping methods. But this would end, as she became very adept to man and his means. She continued to kill and eat, but she learned to leave and never return. Baits with traps no longer worked and she killed more animals than the local ranchers could tolerate. The Departments, both the federal and state, were getting frustrated too. She was becoming a grave concern to all involved, because "The Rustlin' Rogue" was a true cattle rustler and was always on the move to subdue her prey. She needed the 20,000 calories a day that biologist call "hyperphagia," which is gorging in preparation for hibernation. A bear knows exactly where to find it! The Department continued to innovatively set traps, but to no avail. "The Rustlin' Rogue" was making a name for herself! She was very adept and stealthy in her killing.

Mike Madel, grizzly bear biologist for the Department of Fish, Wildlife and Parks on the east slope and who deals with problem bears, said that #316 taught #346 how to kill cattle. She taught others too, which seems to be the consensus. Following are excerpts from the Billings Gazette, in April of 2001, when #346 was finally put down by lethal injection after years of killing cattle. He was twenty-two years of age and near the end of his life. "Mike Madel was called to the Falls Creek area of the east slope in 1987 to inspect a calf that had been killed. A large male grizzly was suspected (#346). A female bear (#316) was responsible for kills in Falls Creek. But in the 1987 case it appeared #346 had picked up on his female counterpart's bad habits. Her number was #316. The next kill was August of 1987 and then another in September. It just continued, said Mike Madel." Rancher Don Converse whose home base is four miles west of Augusta had his encounters too. In the same article I will quote what he said: "But the Falls Creek male wasn't the worst, the female bear #316 was the start of the trouble. She taught him how to eat beef. She taught a lot of other bears too."

When #316 was removed from the ecosystem, bear #346 continued her ways and when he was removed in 2001, after fifteen years of killing cattle, there were (and are to this day) other grizzlies continuing the killings. It all started with #316, the true "Rustlin' Rogue," the kingpin of cattle rustling. She taught the others how to kill and enjoy the treat of prime Montana beef, the very best in protein. Even to this day the Department of Fish, Wildlife and Parks have to pull a bear from that ecosystem. Guess where their bad habits originated?

"The Rustlin' Rogue" would kill, whether it was in close proximity to ranch houses, out in isolated pasture areas, or in feedlots. Her procedure was to kill, eat what she wished, leave and to never return. She knew that staying and guarding her cache was too risky. Once more, returning to claim more food meant traps and snares, which she knew very well in her adolescence. It is hard for me to understand a grizzly not protecting its kill, but she didn't, because she understood the danger zone and sacrificed prime beef in the process. She became very cunning and crafty at avoiding danger, yet she was dangerous because of her seeming lack of fear. Her coyness was evident as she lived in close proximity to man, yet she was never seen. A very wary bear indeed!

Although #316 was a bold bear, she did not let her natural caution minimize. Bears, when tempted by food, will become careless, throw natural caution to the wind and move in to feed. The more the reward, the bolder they become, even with people nearby. #316 simply avoided any prospects of danger, even if the bait looked attractive! She was definitely a smart bear and would be difficult to put down! I was told that she was a very dangerous bear with a fearless disposition. No doubt being a female bear did not help matters, since I have observed their mood swings, more so than the boars, especially when they have cubs. More will be said of her fearless disposition later on in this book.

Her speed and power were displayed by her killings. Breaking necks and vertebrae of cattle is not an easy task. A grizzly that stalks game and then switches the afterburners on to catch and kill them is a frightening display of speed, power and quickness, as she moves with most amazing agility and intensity in fractions of a second. There is no doubt that

34

she put elk down, but she learned that cattle were easier to prey upon. Normally grizzlies will not kill an animal larger than themselves. Since they are versatile in food selection grizzlies resort to easier to obtain food such as carrion and smaller game. According to the experts carrion is easier to digest than fresh meat because it is rotting. Something to do with the enzymes, I believe?

#316 was different, she was not the average grizzly. She loved beef and there was no turning back! Her digestive system was conditioned to fresh beef, a preference to carrion and aged meat. The size of the preyed upon made little difference to her, as she continued her marauding ways. Her sixth sense forewarned her of the inherent danger in returning to her kill sites, therefore she left lots of meat, meat that was left over after her fill. She indeed was the master and the grizzlies she influenced paid their due respect. They no doubt watched her in action and learned first hand, about the how to's, when to's and where to's in satisfying their hunger. Her bad habits were making an impact on the east slope grizzlies.

Word spread state wide, and even throughout the nation of the killings that were happening to cattle and other livestock on the east slope of the Rockies. Most definitely the east slope grizzlies were doing their thing, with "The Rustlin' Rogue" leading the way. Some of the bears were caught and relocated, while others continued. "The Rustlin' Rogue" reminds me of a child in school who gets other children into trouble by being naughty, yet manages to stay out of trouble, at least for a while.

"The Rustlin' Rogue" was predictable in being unpredictable. The ranchers and the Department of Fish, Wildlife and Parks knew she would strike again, but when and where were the million dollar questions. Sometimes they found evidence of her kills, and other times they remained unfounded. Imagine a rancher who just rounded his cattle up in the fall of the year, only to find that several head were missing. When your livelihood depends on numbers and the condition of the cattle, then it really is a set back. The ranchers said that #346 cost them $200,000 when it was all said and done. I wonder what "The Rustlin' Rogue" cost the ranchers, not only by her many kills, but by her influence on other bears in their killings? Even the condition of the cattle needs to be taken into consideration, if they were run a lot by the bears.

Not being a garbage bear helped #316 to be elusive, unlike many of Montana's problem bears that get into trouble because of careless people with their garbage and messy campsites. #316 lived a natural grizzly's life by working to eat. She was not conditioned to living on the welfare of people's garbage, nor was her behavior affected because of being drugged as in the case of a Yellowstone bear that got doped up on PCP, which is angel dust, then proceeded to be a problem. "The Rustlin' Rogue" thrived on cattle, rather than garbage. She invaded feedlots, not cabins. She killed cattle rather than people! #316 was indeed very different!

The ranchers should be appreciated for their patience in their losses. Although they are reimbursed, I doubt whether the money covers the total cost of their losses, perhaps only a fraction. Likewise, the Department needs to be praised for their efforts in trying to minimize the problem by trapping and releasing. The grizzlies are given ample opportunity with this program, so Montana does not become like some other states that have lost their grizzly populations. The book, "Great Montana Bear Stories" tell of the last grizzlies in: Texas—1890, North Dakota—1897, Nevada—1907, California—1922, Oregon—1931, Arizona—1935, and Utah in 1923. The Montana legislature had wisdom in the early 1920's and listed the grizzly with elk and deer as a big game animal. This put controls on the number of bear that could be harvested each year, as determined by sound management studies. Great foresight!

Trying to catch #316, due to her elusive ways, proved to be very costly and ineffective. However, the next problem would be, if she were caught, then what? Would the federal government demand she be released since she had not been caught in her adulthood? Could she be relocated and not come back to the east slope, her "stomping grounds." She proved when she was a sub-adult that the homing instinct was strong, so I doubt that she would stay away. Remember, she is "The Rustlin' Rogue" with a strong homing instinct! The final problem would be to try and catch up with her once again, which seemed almost impossible. After all she was still on the prowl and needed to be caught.

Because a bear is fitted with a radio collar does not make it an easy target! Many of Montana's grizzlies have proven that. The collar is good for giving the Department ideas as the general location where the grizzly travels, but specifically it is difficult to catch up with the great bears. The Giefer bear proved this!

One can somewhat understand the difficulty facing those who were directly affected on the east slope. One thing for certain is "The Rustlin' Rogue" needed to be eliminated, but how, when and where? A roll of the dice had better odds, much better!

Chapter 6
I'm Drawn #1!

In March of 1987 I read in our local newspaper in Kalispell, Montana about a problem grizzly bear damage control hunt to be conducted on the east slope of the Rockies. To qualify one had to put their name, address and phone number on a 3 x 5 card and mail it to the Department of Fish, Wildlife and Parks in Great Falls, Montana. There was no cost involved, other than postage. I told my son, Ladd, that we would stop after school the next day and send our applications for this once-in-a-lifetime opportunity.

Within a day or two after mailing these applications we both completely forgot about the drawings because of the business of the school day and with the extracurricular activities in the later afternoons and evenings.

Late in the afternoon on April 7th, I received a phone call from the press to inform me that I was drawn #1, and Ladd was drawn #3! It did not register with me at first, so I asked, "Number 1 for what?" The person on the other end said, "The Grizzly Damage Hunt!" He congratulated the two of us for being drawn that high, especially out of nearly fifteen hundred applications and from all parts of the country. In the next breath he asked me to call him if a hunt materialized. I more or less laughed, knowing right then and there that I would not be the informer. Would you want the press pressuring you when you're trying to hunt, especially for a grizzly bear? A few minutes later the Department called me to inform us of our good fortune! Good fortune indeed, numbers 1 and 3 out of all those applicants! They were disgusted that the press phoned me first and I cannot say that I blame them. Our conversation led to Mike Madel, a bear management biologist stationed out of Choteau. He would be in contact with me within the next twenty-four hours to lay down the ground rules.

Mike did call that evening, and as we conversed, I knew he was a knowledgeable and highly professional person and that he would be a joy to work with! I will never forget one of his first comments and it went something like this: "Although the grizzly will be wearing a radio collar do not expect this to be a 'turkey shoot'. It will be a real hunt and a very dangerous one, if you have the opportunity. The Department of Fish, Wildlife and Parks will be working against you because we do want to preserve these bears if at all possible." No truer words were ever spoken, as I would learn during the ensuing months. According to the government rules, they would give a male grizzly one chance, and a female two chances to stay out of trouble by transporting them one hundred miles or more with the idea that they would readjust to their new surroundings and stay put. A female is held in higher esteem because of reproduction, which is the reasoning for two chances.

Mike furthered his conversation by asking me to stay by the phone for the next six months, because if a hunt materialized then it would be on a moment's notice. We agreed to talk each week, sometimes many times a week about bear prospects. The season started immediately and would end October 1st when the great bears would be preparing for hibernation. If I missed my call then Mike would call the second person to be given the opportunity, followed by Ladd. If a call never would come then a new lottery would take place the next spring. What would the odds be for Ladd and I to be high in the drawing the second year? Not very good, in fact, near impossible!

Waiting by the phone from April on, with the anticipation of a call for a well-publicized hunt, a hunt that possessed many questions because of its historic nature, would produce tenseness in anyone's diary! Knowing that a hunt may never materialize only made matters worse! Remember, the Department was working against me by giving the bears an ample opportunity to redeem themselves by transporting them that great distance with hope they would adjust to their new habitat. If the great bear continued to be persistent in coming back to the east slope, then a hunt would materialize. It was definitely a long shot for a bear to journey the rugged terrain of the Rockies in a short time, but there was hope. To think that "The Rustlin' Rogue" might be involved was nothing short of lunacy.

During our months of waiting, Ladd and I spent quality time at the rifle range. He became confident with his 30-06 and could put up a good grouping at one hundred yards. I knew my 300 Winchester Magnum very well. A few years previous one of the best gunsmiths custom built it for me to fit like a glove. It had a Mauser action, with a hexagon barrel and a Clairol walnut stock. What an accurate shooting machine, with one-inch grouping at one hundred yards. At two hundred to three hundred yards I was very confident.

Ladd was only twelve, but I was not worried about him. He had gotten his first black bear that spring, while possessing confidence and poise in doing so. During the years past he had been with me on several successful hunts and knew most of the ramifications involved.

When I was gone, Ladd would stay near the phone and when he was gone I would be there ever-listening for the ring. If both of us were gone, which was not too often, my wife, Monica, would do the babysitting.

We did not have cell phones in those days, but if they would have been available then, all of us could have relaxed from this bondage of being tied down.

During the months of waiting, people contacted me from different parts of the country wondering when I would be called. Most definitely the public pressure was mounting for this first-ever east slope Damage Hunt. To make matters worse, the press reminded me to notify them when I was called so they could run more stories. They wanted to come along, as they did during the buffalo harvests in North Yellowstone. This was no buffalo and besides, this was a hunt! A grizzly is dangerously different, besides its habitat is not conducive for the public! Once more, I did not need an entourage when dealing with a wary bear with a sixth sense and the possibility of a deadly attack. Having someone taking notes and pictures, even if they would be left miles away during the hunt, is not glamorous to me. There was enough on my plate and I did not need any other interruptions. Besides, the Department would forbid them to accompany us on this dangerous hunt!

The Department was very encouraging to work with, especially Mike Madel. He was very sensitive to the situation at hand and could empathize with me. Daniel Vincent, the Regional Supervisor for the Department out of Great Falls showed his loyal support during our phone conversations and correspondence, which did encourage me too. The following is one of the letters I received from Daniel Vincent when I was selected number 1:

Dear Mr. Nolin,

You have been selected by computer as number 1 on our roster for a possible grizzly bear damage control action hunt.

If the occasion arises requiring a Grizzly Bear Damage Hunt, you will be contacted by telephone in the order of your ranking on the roster.

Please review the enclosed hunter notification procedure and hunt format and grizzly bear identification brochure.

It is recommended that you use a 30-06 caliber or larger caliber rifle. Should you participate in this hunt, please be aware that we do not imply guarantee for taking or even seeing a grizzly bear.

Sincerely,
Daniel P. Vincent
Regional Supervisor

The Kalispell Daily Interlake paper was one of many papers that published my #1 lottery drawing for this first Damage Hunt. The following is most of that article:

KALISPELL HUNTER HEADS GRIZZLY LIST

A Kalispell man has been picked as the first hunter for a special state hunt for a problem-causing grizzly bear along the Rocky Mountain Front.

Bob Nolin, Superintendent of Flathead Valley Christian School, was the first of 1,389 hunters to be drawn for the special grizzly hunt, the first of its kind in Montana. Ironically, his 12-year-old son, Ladd, was the third hunter drawn by state wildlife officials.

The Montana Department of Fish, Wildlife and Parks received permission earlier this year from the U.S. Fish and Wildlife Service to conduct the special hunt if problems arise. Grizzly bears have caused problems for Rocky Mountain Front ranchers, farmers and beekeepers during recent springs.

Nolin said he sympathizes with ranchers who have problem grizzlies. "I really think the grizzly bear is on the upswing, otherwise I would be very reluctant to hunt for one. I never want to see the grizzly become instinct. I do believe in protecting them."

Most people wanted me to succeed if I was to hunt, but there were some who wanted me to fail. These people just do not understand the total picture of wise game management and the purpose for this hunt if it were to develop. The bear's population is on the incline in Montana, but still protection is necessary. Restricted hunts are a must to keep a healthy grizzly population, along with a healthy fear of man.

As time waned I wondered what I had gotten Ladd and myself into. I did not want Ladd to be hassled by any people with other ideas. After all he was only twelve and did not need that pressure too. I must say that I did a lot of praying and just committing the whole ordeal to the Lord.

The Lord had allowed me to harvest to this point the following big game animals: antelope, whitetail deer, mule deer, elk, black bear, bighorn sheep, moose and mountain goat. Eight of the "Montana Big Ten," now I might have an opportunity for the ninth, Ursus arctos horribilis! However, the pressure for this hunt was beyond my imagination and expectation with all eyes seemingly on me. Not having hunted grizzlies before would definitely shed new light on experiences, especially this unusual experience and after an unusual animal!

I knew I needed to lay public interests, the Department of Fish, Wildlife and Parks, and the ranchers' concerns aside in the very end. It would be the grizzly and me! How would I react? How would the bear react? Under what circumstances would the hunt unfold? Would the mountain terrain be conducive to hunt the great bear, especially a problem one that is adept at avoiding man? Would the landscape be brushy and timber laden, open with mountain peaks, flat or steep? What have I learned through my past experiences to make this hunt successful? These were some of the many questions that I mulled over during the ensuing months.

I reflected on the number of grizzlies that presented themselves to me while hunting, backpacking, fishing, etc. Every one was an awesome creation of the Lord! I cannot remember all the elk, deer, antelope, black bear, big horn sheep, goats and moose that I have seen, but I remember vividly every grizzly! When a person sees one in the wild it will never be forgotten! Besides being awesome, it is majestic and beautiful, just let me say, out of place and out of proportion!

As I meditated on the hunt, it was obvious that I would be after an animal that could turn on me, and in all reality I would be the one being hunted, especially if I were to wound the bear or irritate it somehow. There is no doubt that bear hunting does have an unique allure to it because of the inherent dangers.

I would be challenged mentally, emotionally and physically on this hunt. When hunting I do enjoy the total experience, whether I harvest an animal or not. But mentally, this hunt demanded that the problem grizzly be weeded out for the welfare of the other grizzlies. The weight was on my shoulders and everyone would be taking notice! I knew that I would have to be prepared mentally to tackle such a large chore. A lot of thought and preparation would be necessary.

Emotionally, I could have been a wreck, but I kept my state of mind clear ("The Lord is my refuge.") so my emotions did not run rampant. My mind overruled the emotions, but I had to work at it. Keeping busy with family, friends, school, church, and with all the preparations for this hunt helped to divert the emotional feelings.

Physically, I was in very good shape, due in large part to being physically fit from sports and the outdoors. If the hunt materialized, I felt ready from the physical perspective.

Many hours were spent anticipating the happenings, but more importantly I concentrated on the bear itself. Besides the bear facts from Chapter 4, I also took into consideration the following three characteristics of the great bear: their eyesight is better than one may think. I have heard it said that bears do not see very well. I tend to disagree, their eyesight is near that of a human. They can see movement one half mile away. If the grizzly is not alarmed it will have its head down while feeding; but the moment it lifts its head and looks it can see better than you think. If the opportunity presents itself, I will try to blend in,

hide behind objects, and stalk when the head is down. When the bear lifts its head then I will freeze. A few years ago I watched a grizzly turn rocks over as he as grubbing for food, at over a quarter-mile distance, periodically, he would lift his head and look straight at me! My rig was only a few feet away and tucked behind some brush and trees, so he could not see it. The bear did not hear me or smell me, but he knew I was there the whole time, because he could see me.

When it comes to hearing, I doubt whether there is another animal more keen than the bear. On many black bear hunts I would have to get after guys for walking too noisily. I told them that it was important to softly place each foot down when walking. When walking naturally, upon making contact with the surface of the ground the foot is too loud and the bear will hear the unnatural sound. On different occasions black bears have spooked because my companion was too loud. A grizzly's hearing is just as keen, and I knew being quiet would be necessary if the circumstance presented itself. In addition, my clothes needed to be noise free, since close quarters with the grizzly was a very good possibility. That does not sound good, close quarters with a grizzly!

We even practiced with our rifle bolt actions to be as quiet as necessary so these mechanical mechanisms would not betray us. There was little room for unnecessary noise.

A grizzly's sense of smell, like hearing, is second to none. I read somewhere that a grizzly can smell where a human has walked, for up to forty-eight hours before the scent dissipates! I have had grizzlies sense me with their noses under unbelievable circumstances. Ladd and I watched a grizzly feed at a great distance, and when the bear detected our scent it quickly slipped into some brush. Many cloven hoof animals would never have detected us in that situation, but the great bear did. Most definitely I would have to take into consideration the breeze, or maybe a wind coming off the Rockies. Besides the breeze or wind, the thermals would be taken into consideration. Typically in the morning there will be an updraft, and by later afternoon it will reverse and be a downdraft. I will be constantly checking the air's movement by throwing dust and/or vegetation into the air.

More questions continued to plague me. If I were to get the opportunity, what kind would it be? What would be the distance? Would I shoot off hand, kneeling, sitting, prone or rested over a log, etc.? Would the grizzly be standing and in what direction? The bear could be walking, maybe running, or perhaps laying down? Would I be shooting uphill, downhill or on flat ground? If my shot hit the great bear, would it charge or retreat? Where should my first shot be placed? Would the weather be stormy with poor visibility? Perhaps it would be windy and clear? What time of day would everything unfold and would the sun be a factor? Would I be shooting into the wind, with the wind or crosswind? If a grizzly presented itself, would it be the right bear? Would I have time to set up, or would my opportunity be reflexive? Would the Department personnel be there, and if so, how many? Would I have a backup or would I be alone when, and if, the opportunity presented itself?

I believe you, the reader, are now aware that there were many variables to think about. Hunting elk on my own is one thing, but hunting for a well-publicized grizzly is another. Especially when a multitude of people are waiting for results, one way or another!

If I missed the bear with whatever opportunity I might have, then people I know would forever remember. I certainly would feel that I had let the Department of Fish, Wildlife and Parks down. After all, they put a lot of time into this program. The ranchers would be the biggest concern for a failed opportunity, knowing more cattle would be lost to that bear. Finally, the bears themselves would be hampered by not having these rustlers eliminated. It would make for a more manageable population of non-problem bears.

Wounding the bear would be the worst-case scenario. Immediately I would be placed on the hit-list of people, from hunters to the animal rights activists. Besides I would not want to put those of us who would track the bear in a vicarious position! If tracking was necessary then I would not want to see from the blood sign a yellowish-brown color that looks somewhat greasy, which would indicate a gut-shot. The bear would carry on in pain for some time and be very dangerous to trail, but it would have to be done. I would hope for a bright red and/or frothy red color, indicating a fatal shot to the heart and lungs area. Dark red blood indicates a muscle shot and that would definitely make us on edge when tracking.

If I panicked in a stressful shooting situation, then I would be forever labeled as such. Strange things happen to people in the moment of excitement and none of us are exempt. No doubt about it, I desired steady nerves and a clean accurate shot that would not allow for error and more than anything that the great bear would not suffer. I am a hunter who knows the need for harvesting and not a killer. Wounding an animal and then having it suffer is not the proper way to harvest. A healthy population of the great bears is necessary and removing the problem ones does exactly that; that is why I chose to do this hunt. Besides, I want to emphasize once again that the grizzly population is on the incline in Montana.

The story about "Lenny, the bulletproof bear" had me thinking about bullets. Which bullet should I use and what grain would be best for a grizzly, especially a problem one that may have unnatural adrenaline rushes, which seemed to be displayed by attacking cattle regularly? Adrenalin can make it more difficult to put an animal down, especially a grizzly! Because of the bear's strong bones and thick hide, the bullet would have to be well-built to not fragment upon impact. It would have to be the right grain for my 300 Magnum, with trajectory, velocity and energy that would perform well from one hundred to three hundred yards. After much meditation I decided to stay with my reliable hand loads, the Speed Grand Slam in the 180-grain. Why change now, since I had great success with it? Not once had this bullet fragmented when harvesting many species of large game animals. My load would be 2960 feet per second at the muzzle and 2344 at three hundred yards. My energy in foot-pounds would be 3501 at the muzzle, and 2196 at three hundred yards. The long-range trajectory would drop 7.3 inches at 300 yards. I was comfortable with this total performance and felt if given the opportunity that I could properly harvest this powerful and strong animal, but the bullet would have to be placed well. After all I would be dealing with an animal that can kill a bull or an African lion in seconds!

My hunting gear was always at arm's length and ready for the spur of the moment. I had carefully packed my: rifle, shells, case, optics, footwear, orange hooded outerwear, both warm and cold weather clothing, rain gear, orange cap and daypack. My daypack consisted of the necessary things I always carry in the field: mitts and gloves, knives, sharpener, flashlight, rope, energy bars, drink, tape, first aid, matches, space blanket, compass and extra shells. I always start assembling my equipment with the big three items. They are a good accurate rifle, a sharp knife and good boots.

More and more I was beginning to feel confident. I know it was the Lord, because I had done a lot of praying and meditating on Him. It was His strength and not mine, believe me!

Chapter 7
False Alarm

Sunday, September 6th, I was called by the Department of Fish, Wildlife and Parks and told that a problem grizzly was on the east slope, once again raising havoc with livestock! This was the largest of a pair of problem sub-adult bears and its last chance had culminated. The bears were turned loose on August 7th in the Spotted Bear area of the South Fork of the Flathead River, which is along the northwest border of the Bob Marshall Wilderness. This largest bear headed to the east slope of the Rockies, while the other bear could never be located upon release. This male grizzly reached the Swift Current area on August 31st, then journeyed to Birch Creek. The Department had received permission from landowners to conduct a hunt since the grizzly was on large private ranches. The Department told me to get my gear ready because the call would come Monday morning, and the first Grizzly Damage Hunt in history would take place! I made all the necessary preparations at school to have things in order for me to be gone for most of that week. Then I made all necessary calls to different people, but not the press. Needless to say I was pumped! That night was long because of all the excitement the next day was to offer.

Early Monday morning, Mike Madel flew over the area to receive the final signal of the collared bear. No signal could be detected after many hours of searching. They determined the bear had left the area and would no longer be an immediate problem. The hunt was called off and I was left with mixed emotions. Trying to keep my emotions subjected to my mind was difficult, to say the least. Having my hope built up, then crash, after waiting from April and through the spring and summer and now into September was disappointing! October first was creeping up and my hope for a hunt seemed all but eliminated, because there were no more prospective bears. Even if one materialized, it would be released over one hundred miles away and have to travel through the rugged mountainous terrain to the east slope before October 1st, the end of the season. Not only would the bear have to go over the Rockies, but somehow skirt the Chinese Wall, a steep natural rock formation that extends for miles from north to south in the Rockies. The long strenuous trek before the deadline made my odds, well let's say, not very good!

A teacher friend and I beat the odds and drew one-half curl bighorn sheep tags in the Thompson Falls area of the state. The season began the early part of September so we decided to make preparation for the sheep hunt. I decided to forget the Grizzly Damage Hunt, because it was getting too late in the year. Refocusing was difficult, since I had been geared up for over five months while waiting impatiently by the phone for a call. It was hard to have an opportunity, but the Lord interceded and gave me a peace that did not make sense during these trying times.

Chapter 8
#316 Materializes

On September 8th I received a call from Mike Madel to inform me that grizzly #316 was caught killing cattle! She had eluded the Department for almost three years and was finally caught in the act! Mike was flying in a helicopter over the countryside on the east slope checking bear traps. They saw a grizzly that had just killed a cow, in an open park amidst the timber. The bear was gorging itself on the beef, and upon the appearance of the helicopter the bear broke for the cover of the timber. It was too late, because Mike managed to get a tranquilizing dart in her! When they got to the large female bear it was the notorious #316! Mike expressed excitement to me that they finally caught the "Bear of Bears" and purely by accident! Of all the grizzlies, this was the one they wished for a hunt. However, for her to return to the east slope for such a hunt before the October 1st deadline was only a shot in the dark. Mike was not very optimistic for all this to play out, because he felt she would go into hibernation in the Bob Marshall Wilderness. In fact, he wished she would stay put in the Bob Marshall forever. But of course, that was the whole idea of the program.

There was some glimmer of hope, yet I knew life had to go on. I was not going to sit around and wait any longer. Besides, a busy school schedule, and planning for fall hunts were upon me! This particular fall included: sheep, antelope, deer and elk—in that order. My family and I love wild game meat (much of our sustenance) and what we cannot possibly eat for the year we dole out to the needy. Ladd and I, upon harvest, debone all the meat and then pack it in ice. Try this procedure and you will find that it is a nutritious delicacy.

On September 16th, my hunting companion, Jeff Moser, and I journeyed to Thompson Falls for big horn sheep. Since I had already harvested a full-curl ram and two ewes in previous years, we decided that Jeff would have first opportunity. Two days later Jeff harvested a nice half-curl ram at the very top of a steep rocky mountain. It took several hours from the time we spotted the ram to pull elevation and jockey ourselves into position for a good clean shot. By the time we got to the bottom of the mountain with the deboned meat, cape and horns, it was near 9:00 p.m. We were so exhausted and physically spent, that we decided to drive into Thompson Falls for supper. Cooking at camp did not excite either of us, because we wanted to relax and relive the day's experience without the chore of food preparation and clean up. At the café we would make preparation for my hunt the next day, providing we had any strength left!

After reaching the café, Jeff mentioned that he would call his wife, Arlys, about the day's success. I went to get a booth, from which Jeff was in plain view as he phoned his wife. Excitement permeated his expression as he talked with Arlys. He prematurely hung up and came running back to our booth! He blurted out, "Call Monica right now, #316 is on the east slope killing cattle, and the Department wants you in Choteau for the hunt first thing in the morning!"

Monica had called Arlys, just in case Jeff would call his wife, so the information could be relayed. Great thinking! I quickly phoned Monica and she was very exuberant to forward Mike Madel's information! She told me to call Mike regardless of the time! Immediately, I called Mike to get all the necessary details. He said they wanted to conduct the hunt at eight o'clock in the morning! I told him that we just got off the mountain from sheep hunting and were in Thompson Falls. He agreed to give me an extra hour, but we needed to stage the hunt as quickly as possible! After all, it was "The Rustlin' Rogue," and she was always on the move. Mike expressed disbelief that #316 traveled one hundred and twenty miles over the most rugged terrain in only ten days! She went right back to her killing ways, which did not surprise anyone. Mike made it clear that she was very dangerous! When they released her from the culvert trap that held her for the long and arduous trip back to the Bob Marshall, she chased after the truck for some distance trying to get the Department's personnel! She was enraged indeed! Perhaps she ventured back to the east slope in anger, and was going to retaliate for what they did to her. Maybe she went back to take out her frustration on the cattle. Sounds logical from a human's perspective, but we are dealing with an animal that does not think like us, therefore we really do not know her motivations. More than likely, she was addicted to beef, and wanted more of it before hibernating. Regardless, somehow she skirted the Chinese Wall and continued where she left off in pursuit of cattle! All this happened in just ten days! Once again the pressure was on me, not only because of the "Bear of Bears," but from exhaustion and lack of sleep due to sheep hunting. What a time and place to be called for such an important historic occasion!

After a strenuous day of sheep hunting, we had one hundred and twenty miles to drive to Kalispell, over deer-infested roads. We arrived around 1:00 a.m., took care of the sheep and equipment, cleaned up, and loaded my grizzly hunting gear for the long trek over the Rocky Mountains.

It was 3:00 a.m. and we had another two hundred miles to journey to our destination, which was a certain café in Choteau.

We traveled with very little sleep, in fact, none! Adrenaline helped me overcome the handicapped condition that I found myself in. However, this condition was on the back burner because of the new and sudden adventure.

As we traveled during the night, all Jeff and I could talk about was #316, the Rustler, the Kingpin—and how she could travel that many miles over the rugged mountains called the Rockies in such a short time! We marveled at how she knew which direction to journey! We talked about her boldness, viciousness and unpredictability and that she indeed was the leader and instigator of cattle killing on the east slope! We could not believe that she had finally been caught—by sheer accident—and that I would be hunting for the bear. The bear that demonstrated her power and boldness by killing cattle, whether they were in feedlots or in the pasture!

The pressure was enormous, as I was selected to hunt for her, and now appointed to put her down! Was this even possible? We had to catch up to her first, which had proven impossible the last three years. She was constantly on the move and would roam ten miles per day and more. We would have to hustle, though it seemed impossible to keep up with a bear that seemed to never rest, especially in the mountainous terrain that she called home. Her movement patterns were no doubt influenced by man and his trapping concoctions, yet she was a mover and shaker from birth, which proved to be beneficial for her. Most definitely she was a real adversary, much like the Giefer bear!

How much more climbing could I do? Would the terrain be steep and rocky, brushy and thick, or would we be fortunate to catch her, if we did, on relatively flat ground? Jeff and I talked about every possible scenario, while mixing in her characteristics, during our trek to Choteau. We did mix in a little sheep hunting but not much. Imagine the magnitude of this grizzly hunt, when we had just accomplished a successful sheep hunt and very little was discussed about it, not even my sheep hunt coming up. Normally we sheep hunters would frown on this!

As the sun began to rise in the eastern sky, the Lord's creation illuminated with splendor! His grandeur was evident in the sun's rays reflecting off the tops of the Rockies! The white snow-covered peaks, with the green hue of the timberline that was spotted with yellow and red, due to deciduous trees and bushes turning color from early frosts, was very soothing for me and was timely. Throw in the rock outcroppings, high valleys, and open parks nestled tightly in timber, and a painter's dream came alive!

It was going to be a nice day for the first-ever Grizzly Damage Hunt. The wind was moving from east to west toward the big mountain and from the vast expanse of the plains, where the buffalo once roamed. The sky was clear and the temperature would rise to the low fifties. Could this be an omen for me of better things to come during the day?

Was it possible to actually harvest "The Rustlin' Rogue?" Would we actually be able to outfox her, on her terms, in this first-ever Damage Hunt? Yes, the questions continued to plague me because of the unknowns, and there were many! I was thankful that I had grown accustomed to "pressure situations" in sports. As a quarterback in football, and point guard in basketball (for both high school and college), undue pressure was often upon me. I was the leader in both, and had to make stressful decisions that would not let the teams, coaches, fans and schools down. This was no different, except that my "team" would be two Department personnel (however that would play out) and the "opponent" was #316, an animal that was a killing machine. Because of her unpredictable nature, a game plan was virtually impossible. "X's" and "O's" were of no value now, and to make matters worse, we were going to be on her home turf!

The closer we drove to Choteau, where our rendezvous would take place, the more uncertain I was feeling. For a moment the east slope was not looking too attractive anymore. My mind was elsewhere, as I was imagining every situation possible. During my quiet concentration, I praised the Lord for this opportunity, and all the successful hunts he allowed me to have. A successful hunt is more than getting the animal, it is the total experience and appreciating the Lord for it. But this hunt was different, because I had to get #316! The public demanded it!

When I mulled over in my mind prospective hunting scenarios for #316 during our long night of driving, my obsession always reverted to stalking "The Rustlin' Rogue" in brush and timber then getting a shot as she made a bluff-charge at me. The distance was not that great, maybe seventy-five yards. I shot a couple of more times to anchor her, as she was so strong and determined! Would it be like this, or was this just a figment of my imagination?

We finally arrived at Choteau, and upon reaching our destination in town there were Fish, Wildlife and Parks personnel ready to meet us. More were coming, including a couple of friends of mine from Great Falls to take videos for me. They were Sheldon Schearer and his son Chad,

Photo by Bob Nolin, Billings, MT

who eventually became an elk-bugler champion.   The Department's personnel included: Mike Madel; Bryce Christiansen, backup gunner and Game Warden from Augusta (in case the bear turned on me, or them); Jim Lowe, a mountain pilot who would fly with Mike to initially locate the general area of the bear, if she was still on the east slope; Kerry Constan, the Assistant Game Manager from Great Falls; and Tom Bivins, a Warden in the Choteau area.

After introductions, Mike gave me some bad news, which I was growing accustomed to by this time. He said #316 had moved ten more miles that night and was holed up on the large, remote Salmond Ranch, which was located in the foothills of the Rockies and over twenty miles west of Choteau. The pilot would have to fly to the ranch and receive permission to conduct the hunt from the Salmonds. I was once again set back, because it was a waiting game, wondering if the Salmonds would allow us to trespass on their large beautiful ranch of fifty thousand acres. Patience was the name of the hunt, even from day one in April! I reckoned a couple more hours would not matter, or would it? Perhaps #316 was still on the move, and in that short time she could easily disappear, much like the grizzly from a couple weeks previous. After all, we were dealing with "The Rustlin' Rogue!"

Before noon, Mike and Jim returned with the blessings from the landowners! The hunt was actually going to take place, and the public had no idea what was about to transpire. The press was purposely left out, as to not cause any more tension then what already existed! Only those individuals that rendezvoused in Choteau, plus Daniel Vincent (Regional Supervisor) in Great Falls, and the Salmond family knew what was to unfold! Within twenty-four hours the press would learn of a hunt, and consequently the public would be informed that the historic hunt had taken place. I wondered what the headlines would read? I wished nobody would know, but I knew better, because this hunt was set apart!

Chapter 9
Hunting for the Notorious "Rustlin' Rogue"

The September issue of the 1988 Petersen's Hunting Magazine carried the story of #316, entitled, "Montana's Historic Grizzly Bear Damage Hunt." In the article, I wrote that the long ride to the Salmond Ranch was agonizing and tense! The feelings that engulfed me were reminiscent of an athletic pre-game talk, in that, let us quit talking and get on with it! Let us put the game plan into action! But what was our game plan? We did not have one and we were going against #316, the most formidable foe! Wow! All of the unknowns, and without a game plan, would surely come to fruition, which was the cause for the agonizing and tense feelings!

Once we drove to the cattle crossings of the Salmond Ranch, the entourage was held back. Two wardens, Mike and Bryce, would go with me to the Deep Creek Canyon, where "The Rustlin' Rogue" was supposedly holed up! Jeff was allowed to travel with us to the canyon just in case I could make use of him as a spotter. He would have to be a long way from the bear, a real long way, in case #316 turned on us! It amazed me that the Department let Jeff come along, but I convinced them that he might come in handy as a spotter, stationed high on a cliff above the canyon, and removed from the threat of #316.

Photo by Bob Nolin, Billings, MT

After traveling several miles in the direction of the Deep Creek Canyon, we parked the rig and continued the journey on foot. Finally, we came to the canyon's rim. As I surveyed the steep walls, the adjoining thick brush and trees along the fast moving mountain stream with embedded rock outcroppings and land barriers beneath the rims we were standing on, I remembered Mike's famous words, "Bob, this will be no turkey shoot, it will be a genuine hunt and a dangerous one!" The great bear was holed up in this drainage that also possessed lots of downfall and brush piles. Apparently, the spring runoff that caused the creek to expand its banks caused this jungle of dead brush and trees. After surveying the Deep Creek Canyon, Mike turned to me and said, "Bob, this is your hunt, so you do what you feel necessary." I carefully studied the large and steep canyon once more. I then made note of which direction the stiff breeze was blowing and where the sun was located. I knew if I went to the canyon's floor that my visibility would be greatly impaired.

There was a rock outcropping, nestled above all the canyon hindrances, yet it had adequate visibility because of a small opening between stands of timber. I choose this blitzkrieg site knowing that it was my best opportunity for an ambush, and that it would put me leeward from where we figured #316 was holed up. The opening was nearly thirty yards wide and extended the width of the canyon. The only escape for the cunning bear was to wade in the creek, which would put her behind a cut in the bank that was made from the swift mountain runoff. Otherwise, if the large female crossed elsewhere in this opening then I would see her. My shot would be over two hundred yards—and no doubt running, if she decided to flee her pursuers. Not the most ideal opportunity, but under the circumstances it was the best.

Mike and Bryce consented to walk upwind a mile or more before entering the canyon. They headed northeast and stayed away from the Deep Creek Canyon, so they would not spook her prematurely or move her in the opposite direction. Once they were in place at the bottom of the canyon, slowly but methodically they moved with the wind in my direction. Hopefully #316 would sense them and come my way. I quietly descended, while Jeff stayed on top. I would look at him periodically to see if he saw something I could not. He would give me arm and hand signals if the great bear materialized. Seconds turned into minutes, and the minutes into over an hour, and still no sign of the notorious #316! The tension was mounting with every minute, as I intently studied the landscape! I knew, if my opportunity availed itself, that I would have only a second or two while she hurried across the opening. Still no sign of this mysterious bear! After a couple of hours it became obvious that she had given us the slip! How did she even know I was lurking in the shadows? Maybe it was that before mentioned "sixth sense" that forewarned her. I just knew she moved further up the valley toward the Rockies by traveling in the creek and behind that cut! Wow!

We went a great distance up the canyon to try and head off #316. I repositioned myself in the best location, while Jeff stayed at the top and the two wardens continued to serve as decoys. Now I was roughly two hundred and fifty yards from where I could get an open shot. The

Photo by Jim & Tony Hamilton, Cody, WY

opening had downfall and brush to contend with, but there was no cut in the creek bank for "The Rustlin' Rogue" to be concealed. If she did come my way then I would get glimpses of her as she would move across this small opening. As I sat in wait for this elusive, cunning and intelligent bear, it did not cease to amaze me how she avoided us by using the creek stream and its bank to be concealed during our first failed attempt! How did she know? Now I realized what the Department of Fish, Wildlife and Parks had been dealing with these last years! We were not after the average bear, she was definitely experienced and adept at avoiding man. Two things stood out in my mind at this time: first, she was fleeing upstream with the wind toward the Rockies, and to no man's return; second, she used for her safety the timber, brush and any land forms in the process. It was a game of cat and mouse, and she was winning.

Climbing the walls of the Deep Creek Canyon were beginning to take its toll on me. A taxing sheep hunt from the day before, then no sleep the night between both hunts, added to the problem. Even the night before our sheep hunt there was little sleep, due to the preparation and anticipation. The sun and wind were proving to be adversaries too, as my lips and throat became very dry. The angle of the sun reflected a glare on my glasses and Leupold Rifle Scope, so I turned the bill of my cap and pulled it down somewhat to block the glare from my glasses, which did lessen the overall glare. Periodically I wiped my forehead that was welling with perspiration, due to the sun's glare and from the physical exertion of climbing the canyon's wall. To make matters worse, the earlier stiff breeze increased into a strong crosswind. Most definitely, I did not have the best of conditions, especially at a rough estimate of two hundred and sixty yards, if I even got a shot! All of these variables were taken into consideration as I waited what seemed like an eternity! At least it was not raining!

Once again the minutes increased to over an hour as I quietly waited! Still no sign of #316, the notorious cattle killer! Where was she? Were my decoys (the two wardens) positioned properly to make the great bear come my way, if she was still holed up in the unforgiving canyon? Perhaps she circled them? If she did break out of the timber and cross my predetermined partial opening, what were the chances of even hitting a bear at that great distance, and on the move? I grew up hunting ducks and geese and learned how to lead and follow through, but this was a grizzly and not a bird! She would be jumping downfall, which made for a crooked and not a straight line. In other words, I would not only lead her, but would have to determine the up and down motion too! I did a lot of praying, no doubt about it! I wiped my brow once more then looked up at Jeff to see if he saw the bear? Still no sign of #316! Time was slowly ticking and I had been in position for over an hour! Now I was wondering if there ever was a bear in the Deep Creek Canyon? If there was, it sure fooled me! Maybe she went further up the canyon? Even if a bear came out of the timber and brush below me would it be #316 or another grizzly? I realized at this time how difficult this whole episode was!

I knew my decision would have to be in a split-second, to shoot or not to shoot. My shot would have to be accurate because I would not want to trail a wounded bear, especially this one! I did not worry about mistaking a black bear for a grizzly, because I had hunted enough bears and seen plenty of grizzlies. A black bear is a black bear, while a grizzly is, well you know when you see one!

All my thoughts disintegrated when both Jeff and I caught a glimpse of brush movement! Like a burst of fire from a blowtorch, #316 appeared, running faster than a sprinter, well over thirty miles per hour! Finally the awesome creation of the Lord appeared! The bear that I had heard so much about! Yes, she was as beautiful as Mike said she was! Seven colors adorned her: blond on the back sides and stomach, cinnamon on the face and legs, a touch of black on the flanks and feet, white around the neck, a touch of orange on the back of the neck, silver tipped hairs here and there, and some brown! Wow! A true calico bear! How could a grizzly this beautiful cause so much destruction?

Her long guard hairs were flowing in the breeze as she swiftly hurdled downfall and with little effort, much like a high hurdler! It is hard to describe the feelings one gets when observing a grizzly, but it's out of proportion muscularity leaves a person awestruck.

In the book, "The Grizzly Bear," by Thomas McNamee, the great bear could not be described better. He said, "They are like earth moving equipment that is heavy and stout. Their leg and shoulder bones are almost grotesquely massive. Their skulls resemble river rocks. The muscles on each side of their massive head resemble two flattened footballs. Their jaws can snap a six-inch thick pine tree or a bull's skull like an eggshell! The hump is pure muscle that motors their front legs to dig or kill." And, I will add, to run fast!

It did not seem right to shoot such a marvelous animal, but I knew it had to be done to help preserve the welfare of Montana's increasing grizzly population. Removing these rogue grizzlies, especially #316, would better preserve innocent grizzlies, because they would not be subject to her bad habits. No doubt about it, the east slope grizzlies would have a better reputation without her.

My confidence returned as I put the cross hairs of my 9X Leupold on the bear and naturally followed through to a point two feet in front of her nose. Considering the speed at which the cattle rustler was running, I knew there would be one shot—and one shot only! Over the years I had taken many game animals on the run, but a grizzly, especially this one! I squeezed off the 180 grain Grand Slam Handload and it found the mark on the base of #316's neck! She somersaulted four times and ended up on a pile of washed up brush from the creek! There was no thrashing, clawing, or biting! Jeff came crawling down the embankment, ecstatic and yet not believing that I had even hit the bear. He was yelling repeatedly, "I've never seen a shot like that!" As I carefully studied the great bear through my scope, I put another assurance round into her. We found out later that it was not necessary, because my running shot had hit her in the spine, causing an instant and merciful death.

It took us ten minutes to climb down the embankment and wade through brush and downfall to the notorious #316! I could hardly wait to see the bear up-close, and when I did, I just stared at the large beautiful female, with a trickle of tears in each eye. It was hard to fathom that five feet from me was the kingpin of cattle killers! In time, Mike and Bryce came out of the brush to join Jeff and I. The four of us just stared and said nothing. Finally, I had the guys remove their caps, then a prayer of gratitude was said to the Lord for his beautiful creation, and that I was so blessed to have this opportunity. (I always thank the Lord for the animals he has allowed me to harvest, and for animals that people harvest while they are with me on a hunt.) After prayer, congratulations and more thought, Mike said he was relieved the killer was dead, and yet he had grown accustomed to her ways and felt it was unfortunate that such a prime sow had to be removed from the population. I felt the same emotions, but the relief that it was finally over was indescribable!

Photo by Bob Nolin, Billings, MT

After most of the numbness left, the other people who were waiting miles away at the entrance of the Salmond Ranch, were notified. In short order they arrived along with one of the owners. If there was one word to describe the whole atmosphere at that time it would be "unbelievable!"

Remarkably, the spur of the moment game plan worked to a "tee!" Having Mike and Bryce in position for #316 to wind them, worked!

Jeff, being high up at the edge of the canyon was also beneficial. I positioned myself at the correct elevation for the sake of visibility, any lower and #316 would have escaped unseen, and continued her cattle killing ways. Had I been higher, my 260-yard shot would have been further. After all, the shot was too far in the fist place!

Photo by Bob Nolin, Billings, MT

Photo by Bob Nolin, Billings, MT

Photo by Bob Nolin, Billings, MT

Chapter 10
Conclusion

Contemplating the hunt, I have to appreciate the Department of Fish, Wildlife and Park's efforts to try and save grizzly bears. Mike Madel's warning, "The Department will be working against you," was obvious throughout the months of waiting. They did give the grizzlies every chance to stay out of trouble. Staging the hunt made it clear that all options for the bear to survive had been eliminated. Finally, they allowed me to mastermind the hunt, for which I am appreciative.

Bear #316 is now fully mounted in a glass case. Although I own her, I opted to display her at St. Mary's Lodge, at the St. Mary's entrance of Glacier National Park. She is positioned in a natural pose, with her two back legs on the bottom of the case. One of her front legs is on a piece of juniper driftwood, which is native to the East Front. The other leg is up, with her paw reaching out in the direction she is gazing. She is looking for her next meal, and ready to move on in her "Rustlin' Rogue" fashion. A cow skull is on the floor of the case, which signifies another of her kills.

The Grizzly Damage Hunt was well thought through by the government. They believed eliminating the problem bears, especially the

Photo by Bob Nolin, Billings, MT

culprits, would enhance the rest of the population. It was good judgment to allow a hunter to do this, and it was a typical hunt with all the strategies, unknowns, guesswork, stamina, exertion, prayer, etc, but non-typical with the enormous public pressure! It was different hunting with officials, rather than my hunting buddies (other than Jeff). But I enjoyed them and their professionalism.

The Grizzly Damage Hunt continued for one more year. A man from one of the eastern states was drawn number one. He had done a lot of hunting too, but when he saw a grizzly, panic set in when true grit was needed! He put himself in a risky situation, but he walked away unscathed and so did the bear! Shortly thereafter, the grizzly was put on the endangered list, consequently there will be no more grizzly hunting in Montana. So ended the Grizzly Damage Hunt, with #316 being the historic bear. She was the only one ever taken on this particular hunt, but the bear that should have been eliminated from the ecosystem was, to the credit of the other grizzlies and all the people involved. She would no longer influence the other grizzlies in her cattle rustlin' ways!

Another amazing fact concerning the mysterious life of the cunning and crafty bear is that she bore no scars! Why is this amazing? Because she killed cattle and she did it in such a fashion that the horns or any other part of the bovine's body barely touched her. Even a grizzly will bear scars from killing an animal larger than they, especially many such kills. She apparently did the killing in such a quick and forceful manner that the beef had no chance whatsoever to kick, throw its head, or twist its body, which could cut and bruise the assailant. She did break the necks of many bovine, telling me that she did it with one blow, much like the knockout punch in boxing, without being hit at all!

Her hide was in perfect condition despite her lifestyle, but her claws were worn down three-quarters of an inch, caused by the long trek from the Bob Marshall Wilderness and over unforgiving rocky and steep terrain. It is possible that she made the journey in less than ten days. We know she had killed a cow the day before the hunt, but maybe she had arrived a day or two before this first kill. Then again, maybe this was not her first kill after arriving on the east slope.

Concerning her beauty; I had talked about it earlier, but to have the Department personnel make comments about it, while Jeff and I were skinning her for a life-size mount, was most exhilarating. They said, and in no uncertain terms, that she was the most beautiful grizzly they had seen! That was an honor to hear from officials who know, because of their numerous dealings with the great bears. With all the grizzlies that I have seen, I can vouch for their statement. Besides the many colors that adorned her, a feature that stands out is the dark markings around her eyes and nose that give a distinguished mask-like appearance, almost like "The Lone Ranger!"

Grizzlies are solitary for most of their lives, but when they do associate with other bears then the dominant ones stand out. Because #316 stood out, she definitely was the alpha, and both the Department of Fish, Wildlife and Parks and the ranchers could testify to this fact. What was it that placed her at this pinnacle of dominance? Was it her disposition? Was it her boldness? Perhaps it was her intelligence? Just maybe her overall characteristics that she utilized placed her above the rest? Whatever the case, #316 was independent and did her own thing in a masterful way.

There is so much we do not know about #316, but what we do know is that she was indeed a bear that should be placed in the archives, along with the likes of other Montana grizzlies that became famous for one reason or another. After all, she did teach #346 how to kill livestock and he became famous! No doubt about it, "The Rustlin' Rogue" was a legend in her time!

To fathom how dominant man is and the position he holds in the food chain, that an animal like #316 even exists today, causes man to take a step back in wonderment. The great bear's characteristics (which were discussed earlier) and how they utilize them are just mind-boggling! It is a blessing for us that the Lord created within the great bears a fear and/or respect for man. Otherwise we would be in trouble, because they would be feasting on us rather than on cattle!

Since we are talking about man's respect for the great bears, the following should be discussed and implemented: almost sixty percent of human/grizzly conflicts are due to man encroaching on the bear's turf. If you do take to the wilderness, then follow a basic rule, that is: "keep your campsite clean" from food scent of stored food and/or garbage. When Ladd, his friend Matt, and I went Dall sheep hunting in the Brooks Range of Alaska we put our food (dried) in containers that were 14"x8," and round, so they were easy to pack. A bear could not break into them because they would roll in their mouths and were virtually impossible to pick up. These metal containers are supposed to be airtight so the bears cannot smell the contents. We even hauled them fifty yards from camp each night for further precaution. Finally, properly dispose of leftovers and keep your dishes clean. If this set of rules were followed more often, the sixty percent would be reduced significantly. Both man and beast would benefit immensely, which is what all of us wish for!

Chapter 11
A Biblical Analogy

Getting back to #316, when I stared at the large sow as she lay still on the ground, I had mixed emotions. Looking at a prime female that was pushing six years of age and being eliminated from the population really was disheartening. Yet, I had to focus on the fact that she was the notorious cattle killer and that other bears would live because of her death.

This brings us to an important matter, and the next few paragraphs will speak of that. The great bear #316, blends so well with one of my favorite Bible verses in the book of John. In God's "Word," which is also #316. In John chapter 3 and verse 16 God's Word says this: "For God so loved the world, that he gave his only begotten Son, that whosoever believeth in him should not perish, but have everlasting life." Just think the God of the universe loves you (the reader of this book) with a love that is unfathomable! No matter what you may think of yourself, nor the sins you may be in or have been involved with, God loves you. This love is called "unconditional love." Regardless of your history, God takes you where you are now! You might say, "Show me this love." Well, God has shown it to you by giving you a gift, and not just any ordinary gift, but

His best and perfect gift! You might say, "Well, what is this gift?" This gift is "Jesus Christ," God's only Son! You might say, "Well, what is the purpose for this gift to me?" The purpose is this: since God is a perfect God and He lives in a perfect place called heaven, and since you and I are imperfect (remember the sin) and our destination is hell (the Bible is clear on this), it is impossible for us to be in heaven even one day. But God in His wonderful display of love has made it possible for us to go to heaven! God's perfect plan for us to do that is simple, and this brings us to the question, "What is a gift?" Your answer should be, "Something that is given to me. I do not have to earn it, but I have to receive it." Well, that is exactly it! God gave us His only Son, Jesus Christ, that whosoever will receive Him will have their sins forgiven, and inherit eternal life (heaven) one day. Would you like to receive Him, God's gift to you? If yes, then pray the following prayer by reading slowly and with meaning: "Dear God, I am a sinner and wish to turn away from these sins that I have committed. I believe what your book the Holy Bible says, that if I receive your gift, that is Jesus Christ, then I can be forgiven of my sins, and inherit heaven one day when I die. I do receive Jesus Christ and invite Him to come into my life. Now my sins are forgiven. I believe your Word, the Holy Bible, that Jesus Christ took my sins on Him when He died on the cross. He was my sacrifice, he took my place, and now He has made me forgiven and acceptable in your sight. Thank you, my God and Father, for your Son who is now my savior! Amen!"

If you have prayed the above short prayer with earnestness, please sign and date the following lines. This will always be a remembrance for you that you have invited God's only son, Jesus Christ, to come into your life to forgive you of your sins. Only through Jesus Christ can your sins be forgiven, because He took your place, bore your sins and died in your place on the cross some two thousand years ago. He rose from the dead after three days and now He lives at the right hand of His Father (God). When you invite Jesus Christ to come in and forgive you, He does! He tells His Father that you are now forgiven and He marks you down in His Book, called "The Lamb's Book of Life." If you blow it by sinning again, remember that you are forgiven, but He wants you to confess it. That is, tell Him that you sinned and carry on with your life. You will find yourself not wanting to sin, and it will bother you when you do.

Get yourself a Bible and begin to read in the book of St. John. I always tell people who have just been saved from their sins through Jesus Christ to read this book in the Bible. St. John tells of the life of our Lord Jesus Christ, which will give you a better understanding of Him. Look in the table of contents for the page number. You can get a Bible in a Bible bookstore. I use the King James print of God's Word, so ask for that. Start attending a church that teaches God's Word accurately. There are many churches to stay away from, because they have the appearance of teaching correctly but stray from the truth. In time, the Lord will show you if they deviate from the Bible. It is important for you to learn the Word of God (the Bible) so you can mature in the Lord's direction for your life. Having a Christian friend to have fellowship with is also important.

For those of you who prayed the prayer with meaning, please fill in these lines:

_____

Name

_____

Date I invited Jesus Christ to forgive me of my sins
and save me from hell and unto heaven.

I hope you enjoyed reading this book about #316. I enjoyed writing it, especially about an animal that I highly regard. I have always said, that God created animals and then He created "Ursus arctos horribilis!" Only we humans are created in His image, and are higher up on the food chain. Therefore, it is important to be wise stewards of our grizzly population.

Sources

Lapinski, Mike. True Stories of Bear Attacks. West Winds Press, Portland, Oregon. 2004.

Long, Ben. Great Montana Bear Stories. Riverbend Publishing, Helena, Montana. 2002.

McMillion, Scott. Mark of the Grizzly. Falcon Publishing, Inc., Helena, Montana. 1998.

McNamee, Thomas. The Grizzly Bear. The Lyons Press, New York. 1982, 1984, 1997.

Nolin, Robert. "Montana's Historic Grizzly Bear Damage Hunt." Petersen's Hunting, Petersen Publishing Company, Los Angeles, CA. 1988.

Russ, Tony. Bear Hunting in Alaska. Northern Publishing, Wasilla, Alaska. 2004.

Other Sources of information:

"Euthanized Grizzly Legendary Cow-Killer." The Billings Gazette, 28 April 2001.

"Kalispell Hunter Heads Grizzly List." The Daily Inter-Lake, Kalispell, Montana. 26 April 1987.

"Grizzly Hunt's Target Bear Disappears." The Great Falls Tribune, Great Falls, Montana. 15 September 1987.

Holy Bible. The King James Version. Genesis and John.

About the Author

Photo by Bob Nolin, Billings, MT

Bob Nolin is one of a handful of hunters to have harvested the "Montana Big Ten" game animals. Those animals include: antelope, whitetail deer, mule deer, elk, black bear, moose, bighorn sheep, mountain goat, mountain lion and grizzly bear. Presently the grizzly is delisted so there are nine species. Besides Bob's phenomenal success in Montana, he has successfully harvested game animals in Alaska, South Dakota and Minnesota.

Bob is a former educator, and presently a Christian counselor. In his leisure time Bob enjoys writing about his outdoor endeavors. He has written articles for various hunting magazines, and most recently wrote "A Hunter's Devotional Thoughts" booklet. He is in the process of writing devotionals on each of the Montana "Big Ten Game Animals." He has spoken at numerous outdoor fellowship groups and banquets about his hunting adventures, while incorporating his faith in Jesus Christ.